# Novels for Students, Volume 58

Project Editor: Kristen A. Dorsch Rights Acquisition and Management: Ashley Maynard, Carissa Poweleit Composition: Evi Abou-El-Seoud

Manufacturing: Rita Wimberley

Imaging: John Watkins

©2018 Gale, A Cengage Company

ALL RIGHTS RESERVED. No part of this work covered by the copyright herein may be reproduced, transmitted, stored, or used in any form or by any means graphic, electronic, or mechanical, including but not limited to photocopying, recording, scanning, digitizing, taping, Web distribution, information networks, or information storage and retrieval systems, except as permitted under Section 107 or 108 of the 1976 United States Copyright Act, without the prior written permission of the publisher.

Since this page cannot legibly accommodate all copyright notices, the acknowledgments constitute an extension of the copyright notice.

For product information and technology assistance, contact us at **Gale Customer Support, 1-800-877-4253.**

For permission to use material from this text or product, submit all requests online at www.cengage.com/permissions.

Further permissions questions can be emailed to **permissionrequest@cengage.com** While every effort has been made to ensure the reliability of the information presented in this publication, Gale, A Cengage Company, does not guarantee the accuracy of the data contained herein. Gale accepts no payment for listing; and inclusion in the publication of any organization, agency, institution, publication, service, or individual does not imply endorsement of the editors or publisher. Errors brought to the attention of the publisher and verified to the satisfaction of the publisher will be corrected in future editions.

Gale
27500 Drake Rd.
Farmington Hills, MI, 48331-3535

ISBN-13: 978-1-4103-6557-6
ISSN 1094-3552

This title is also available as an e-book.
ISBN-13: 978-1-4103-9288-6
ISBN-10: 1-4103-9288-6
Contact your Gale, A Cengage Company sales

representative for ordering information.

Printed in Mexico
1 2 3 4 5 6 7 22 21 20 19 18

# *The Underground Railroad*

Colson Whitehead 2016

## Introduction

American author Colson Whitehead, whose first novel was published in 1999, has intrigued readers anew with every book written since, constantly adapting, mixing, and even creating new styles, genres, and perspectives. From dystopian future to folkloric past, from soft nostalgia to raging zombies, he writes as if capable of anything.

What he was not always certain he was capable of—or ready for—was a slave narrative, for which he would have to confront a past, full of cruelty and violence, that most African Americans would prefer to leave behind. He had the seed of an idea for a narrative twist on the Underground Railroad back in 2000, but it would take him fifteen years to bring the novel revolving around that idea to full fruition. Quite literally taking the reader to new places in the history of slavery, by novel means, *The Underground Railroad* (2016) stands out for its inspired use of fantasy in a way not at all trivializing the tragedies of the horrible institution. He is especially concerned with readers' realizing not only how horrific slavery was back then but also how the institution has echoed over the years since then, through the twentieth century and beyond. Since part of Whitehead's intent is to fill in the blanks that white versions of slavery too often gloss over, the novel features appalling levels of violence —just as the South did—conveyed just graphically enough to make the circumstances clear, and as such is best suited to mature readers. *The Underground Railroad* won both the 2016 National Book Award and the 2017 Pulitzer Prize.

## Author Biography

Arch Colson Chipp Whitehead was born on November 6, 1969, in Manhattan, New York City. He traces his roots through a grandmother who arrived from Barbados—home to many a sugarcane plantation—in the 1920s and a grandfather who descended from Virginia slaves. That grandfather came to own a chain of funeral homes in New Jersey, making death a common around-the-house subject for Whitehead's mother. The family grew to appreciate horror films, and one of Whitehead's earliest literary inspirations was a Stephen King novel. He also adored X-Men and Spider-Man comics and other fantasy and science fiction works. In high school, he shifted gears upon realizing how powerful literary fiction could be, admiring writers ranging from the traditional novels of Charles Dickens and Fyodor Dostoyevsky to works by Ralph Ellison and Thomas Pynchon.

While in high school, Whitehead had the experience of being racially profiled. Minding his own business in a convenience store, he was approached by a police officer, handcuffed, and brought outside: a lady had been mugged just blocks away, and Whitehead was perhaps the first black teenager the police found. The victim immediately declared that Whitehead was not the culprit, and he was released. He would later acknowledge that he had been prepared for such an incident by his father, who realized the danger that can face African Americans traveling alone in white communities, or anywhere. The father also helped empower his son afterward by pointing out that it was within his rights to demand the officer's badge number, to report to the officer's superiors if appropriate.

Whitehead graduated from Trinity School and then, in 1991, from Harvard University, where he majored in English. He went on to obtain his dream job, writing for the *Village Voice* as a cultural critic, able to mix references to the likes of French philosopher Jacques Derrida with analysis of the music of Grandmaster Flash. His first attempt at a novel, a satirical treatment of young-adult life in New York City, was so unimpressive as to cause him to lose his agent. But new inspiration would strike—while he was watching a TV program about defective escalators—leading to the publication of his first novel, *The Intuitionist*, a thrilling fable about a rogue elevator inspector, in 1999. Both his debut and his next several novels won critical acclaim, nominations, and awards, and in 2002 he was awarded a MacArthur Foundation "genius grant."

In addition to his novels, Whitehead has written nonfiction books about New York City and about the World Series of Poker. *The Underground Railroad*, published in 2016, is his sixth novel. His essays and reviews have appeared in periodicals including the *New York Times, Harper's, Salon, Spin*, and *Newsday*, and he has taught at a variety of universities, including New York University,

Wesleyan, Columbia, and Princeton. Whitehead lives in Brooklyn with his wife, photographer Natasha Stovall, whom he met at the *Village Voice*, and their two children.

## Plot Summary

*The Underground Railroad*'s twelve chapters follow a pattern, alternating between short chapters named for people and long chapters named for places. Each long chapter opens with a notice about an escaped slave—not anyone in the novel (until the final notice)—sometimes offering a reward.

## Media Adaptations

- An audiobook version of *The Underground Railroad*, available on CD or for digital download, was produced by Books on Tape in 2016, read by Bahni Turpin, with a running time of eleven hours.

## *Ajarry*

Cora's grandmother, Ajarry, was kidnapped as a girl when her entire West African village was enslaved. Her family members died along the way to America, where she was sold from owner to owner until ending at the Randall plantation in Georgia. There, Cora has been asked twice by Caesar to escape with him: first she said no; three weeks later, she said yes.

## *Georgia*

It is Jockey's "birthday," a regular (if not exactly annual) celebration for the slaves on the northern half of the Randall plantation. Cora sits by her inherited garden plot, while the young girl Lovey prepares to enjoy the evening. The plot, three square yards, was passed from Ajarry (now deceased) to Mabel (who escaped) to Cora. However, Ava covets the plot and has Moses, a slave enforcer, move Cora to a building called the Hob, home to the outcast slaves. Still, Cora clings to her plot.

A domineering slave named Blake arrives and builds a doghouse on Cora's plot. Cora immediately smashes the doghouse with a hatchet. Blake gives up the space, but he and his fellows spread gossip about Cora, and the others later rape her.

Jockey's party proceeds with races—Chester is the fastest boy—music, and dancing. Then James Randall arrives, hoping a slave named Michael can give a recitation of the Declaration of Independence for James's brother Terrance. Learning that Michael is dead, Terrance insists that James's slaves dance for him. They do so, but in the commotion Chester causes a drop of wine to stain Terrance's white shirt. Terrance beats Chester savagely. When Cora intervenes, he beats her too.

Two weeks later, a woman named Nag is still tending Cora's wounds from the whipping that followed that incident. Soon James falls ill and dies, and the tyrannical Terrance inherits the northern half of the plantation. While Terrance is away in New Orleans, Big Anthony escapes, but he is caught. Caesar approaches Cora for the second time about escaping, but she still declines. Terrance has Big Anthony publicly tortured to death for three days, punctuated by a speech to the slaves—and a silent signal to Cora, effectively claiming her as his mistress.

Cora, now ready to escape, approaches Caesar. He has been in contact with a white man named Fletcher, whose house is thirty miles away and who will support the escape. The following night they flee, going west through swampland and then heading northeast. Lovey appears; she figured out the pair's plotting and followed them. Passing near a road around dawn, they proceed through wilderness and then sleep until the evening. When they resume travel at night, past farmland and onto a hog trail, they encounter four white men. Caesar fights one off, and Cora injures one—only a boy—with a rock and knocks him out. Lovey is dragged off by the other two.

Caesar and Cora continue their journey and reach Fletcher's house. There, they learn that Lovey's absence had led to an early alarm over the runaways, but the slave hunters had lingered in the swamp. The twelve-year-old boy whom Cora struck has not regained consciousness. Fletcher hides the two in his cart, passes through a town, and takes them to a barn full of chains and shackles made for slaves. A trap door leads to a tunnel—and a subterranean train station. An engine with a rickety boxcar arrives, and Caesar and Cora are driven away. They surface in South Carolina.

## *Ridgeway*

Ridgeway's father was such an impeccable role model that Ridgeway could not live up to the precedent. At the age of fourteen, he became a slave patroller, hunting runaways. After visiting New Jersey, he drifted north to New York City, where hunting was more of a challenge. When Ridgeway's father died, he returned to Virginia, now a feared slave catcher with a gang. He was summoned to Randall to track down Mabel, but failed; now, vengeful, he is summoned to track down Cora.

## *South Carolina*

Life at the Andersons' follows a comfortable daily routine, with Bessie watching over the two Anderson children. After work, she walks home to the city dormitory, puts on her new dress, has dinner, and chats with Miss Lucy, who is in charge of the women's dormitory. Bessie—the new alias of Cora—arrived months earlier via the underground railroad, received by Sam. According to their forged documents, she and Caesar are now considered property of the government, which is buying up slaves and depositing them in South Carolina.

Cora is getting educated, and school on Saturday morning is painstaking. Three weeks after arriving, recalling her mother's escape, she had asked Miss Lucy if there were any records of her, but there were not. When Cora first arrived, she played the part of Bessie well, though the doctor's appointment made her feel dehumanized. Now, a few months into her stay, Cora prepares for an evening social, expecting to see Caesar there. At the event, he tells her that another train of the underground railroad will be coming in a few days. When the first train came, they were just getting settled; feeling more comfortable as time passed, they declined the next two trains as well—and now they want to stay. At midnight, a frantic, half-dressed woman runs outside screaming that her babies are being taken from her; she is gradually subdued.

Miss Lucy congratulates Cora on being specially recommended for a new job at the Museum of Natural Wonders. There, Cora learns that she will take turns with two other women performing parts to enliven three historical displays: primitive Africa, a slave ship, and a plantation.

Meanwhile, a new hospital has opened, but Cora finds her visit there unsettling: Dr. Stevens strongly advises her to undergo sterilization and to urge her peers to get sterilized as well. Given a full tour of the museum, Cora becomes more conscious of the history-skewing inaccuracies. At the dorms, she learns that the women from number forty—which is, like Hob on the plantation, a place for outcast and disabled women—have been transferred to the hospital.

Caesar and Cora meet Sam, a station agent, at his house, where he reports that the hospital is deceiving the black men who go to Red's, a saloon, so that they can study the effects of untreated syphilis. At the museum, tired of insulting looks and words from white people, Cora starts glaring back through the glass at some, frightening them. She asks Miss Lucy about the women from number forty and is told they are not coming back, having moved on to elsewhere. Cora also overhears that someone—a slave catcher—is looking for murderers. She hurries to Caesar's dorm, but he is still at work. She then goes to a bar, where Sam signals to meet her in the alley; two men from Ridgeway's gang are inside. She goes to Sam's house, and in a hour he follows and lets her underground. Sam goes back out to look for Caesar. Soon, Cora hears commotion overhead and realizes the house is being ransacked, then burnt down.

## *Stevens*

Studying at a third-rate medical school in Boston, Stevens works the night shift at the Anatomy House to support himself while in school. His other purpose is to let in the body snatchers who supply the school with cadavers for study. Stevens also likes to go along with Carpenter and his assistant to dig up the bodies. With high competition in the shadow economy for dead bodies, Carpenter focuses exclusively on unguarded African American graveyards. Stevens dreams of studying the living just as he studies the dead.

## *North Carolina*

The train Cora expects does not come, and alone underground she grows dehydrated, weak, and unbalanced. Finally a train does arrive—passing straight through the tunnel at first, as the fifteen-year-old driver did not expect her and is confused. For a passenger car, it has only an open platform with straps. The ride is turbulent.

Left at a rock-walled mountain station, Cora finds, instead of an exit tunnel, only a landslide. Despairing, she sleeps, and is awakened by the station agent, Martin Wells. He reports that the station is closed but hides her in his cart, drives along the "Freedom Trail"—dotted by lynched black bodies as far as the eye can see—and to his home. There, his wife, Ethel, angry, helps hide Cora in a tiny space above a false ceiling in the attic. While their maid, Fiona, works around the house, Cora must stay there all day, descending from the attic only late at night for a meal and chat with Martin. Through a peephole in the outer wall, she watches the goings-on in the town park—all white people. The Friday Festival features entertainment leading up to the ritual appreciation of the night riders, led by a man named Jamison. A new member of the group has found and captured a black woman, who is hanged as the highlight of the weekly festival.

Martin tells Cora about the patrollers and regulators, who have all the authority of police. A meeting of North Carolina's decision makers, including Jamison, had led to the decision to start importing poor Europeans—Irish and Germans—so as to replace the black population as laborers, allowing them to be genocidally eliminated. By law, all colored people in North Carolina are subject to exile or death. As weeks, then months, pass in the attic, Cora endures stifling heat and grows thinner. She reads almanacs and the Bible to pass the time. Martin insists that with the station closed, any escape effort is doomed. She fantasizes about life in the North.

The summer solstice is a week away. One week before that, Cora had spilled her chamber pot, though luckily Fiona either failed to notice or ignored the problem, and Martin later cleaned it up. When the regulators visited and searched the house later, the attic still smelled rank—Martin blamed raccoons. They hear news that just that morning, a white husband and wife were hanged for harboring two black boys. That night, Cora grows ill and must be brought down to a bedroom, where Ethel cares for her. Fiona is dismissed for the week, so that she does not discover Cora, on the pretext of Martin's being seriously ill. While Cora is ill, Ethel reads aloud to her from the Bible, leading Cora to argue over what it says about enslavement. Cora is still in a bedroom when the Friday Festival is interrupted by the regulators' knock on the front door. Cora scrambles to get away, but she is caught and brought to the front porch. Before the mob can take action and hang her, Ridgeway claims her. As they leave, Cora sees Martin and Ethel being stoned to death by the crowd.

## *Ethel*

At age eight, Ethel was happily playing subordinating games with her family's slave girl, Jasmine—such as missionary and African native—but her father made the games stop. When Jasmine was fourteen, after her mother's death, Ethel's father started visiting Jasmine upstairs. Later Jasmine was sent away, leaving the lonely Ethel to nurture dreams of being a savior to heathen Africans. Having Cora in North Carolina was her big chance.

## *Tennessee*

Ridgeway proceeds with his gang through Tennessee, having also picked up a runaway named Jasper, who sings incessantly and annoyingly. They cross miles of land destroyed by wildfire, which left poor whites looking like runaway slaves. Cora is in chains, but still she has tried to run twice. They are not going straight to Georgia but instead west, in pursuit of another runaway. Ridgeway tells Cora of meeting with Terrance Randall and of Lovey's death. Caesar was traced through Mr. Fletcher and then Lumbly. Jasper sings one time too many, and Ridgeway kills him.

After passing beyond the burnt towns, the gang approaches a town marked by signs warning of a yellow fever quarantine; they pass around it. Cora counts her misfortunes. Finally reaching an accommodating, if rowdy, town, they stop. Here, Homer, a young former slave who has stayed with Ridgeway out of a strange loyalty, buys Cora a dress and tells her to change. Ridgeway takes her out for supper and finally tells her of Caesar's death. He drunkenly tells her his views of life, even continuing his speech through the door as she uses the outhouse. Back at the wagon, Boseman fears the fever's reach and insists they camp outside town. In the night, Boseman wakes Cora up, wanting her, and she assents in the hope of escaping. When they exit the wagon, Ridgeway ambushes Boseman and beats him in punishment—but then three black men, with two guns and a knife, appear and start giving orders. Homer throws the lantern at them, and the black leader shoots at Ridgeway but misses. In the ensuing fight, Boseman is mortally wounded, and the rifleman (Red) chases after Homer. Cora subdues Ridgeway by strangling him with her chains, and they lock him to the wagon. Homer has disappeared, so they hasten to leave. Cora gives Ridgeway three kicks in the face.

## *Caesar*

In a flashback to Jockey's birthday celebration, Caesar watches the races from the schoolhouse, where he gets away to read in privacy. He thinks of his parents' unpleasant enslaved fates. Cora's brave defense of Chester convinces Caesar of what he already suspected—that he needs her in order to escape successfully.

## *Indiana*

Now living on the Valentine farm in Indiana, Cora feels as if she is behind in the school led by Georgina, where she studies alongside mostly young black children. She accompanies Molly back home, past the pig roasting, where Cora, Molly, and Sybil share a cabin. They spend time quilting. Royal (one of the three men who had helped Cora escape from Ridgeway) is three days late coming back from a recent excursion. Cora asks Sybil and others about Mabel, but no one knows her. The hogs are the highlight of the Saturday barbecue, after which the children are taken to play games and the adults have political discussions. Gloria Valentine brings up the possibility of moving the community farther west. Then Rumsey Brooks reads some poetry. When a dance starts, Cora leaves for her cabin—and finds Royal there. He has a black eye, but also a new almanac for Cora.

A month after Cora arrived, in August, Royal took her to the nearby ghost tunnel—an underground railroad station with only a handcar, leading to an unknown destination. The rest of the night of Cora's rescue, the stories of the three men involved, and the underground railroad ride from Tennessee are all recounted.

In November, Sam arrives, alive after all, and reports that Terrance Randall is dead. Ridgeway and Homer are said to have permanently retreated to a cave. The farm holds a corn-shucking bee, which is won by Mingo's team. Cora gets engrossed in the new library, where she is once visited by John Valentine for a chat. A big meeting will take place soon, with Lander and Mingo both present, to discuss Indiana's increasing—and increasingly threatening—white population.

The big meeting—the farm's last—happens on a chilly December night. In turn, John Valentine and Mingo speak, but while Lander speaks, he is shot. Whites have gathered and surrounded the building, and when Royal rushes to help Lander, he is also killed. The farm's buildings are burned down. As Cora looks for Molly, Ridgeway seizes her. Homer is also there, and he had heard the dying Royal mention to Cora a tunnel.

## *Mabel*

Tired of submitting to the vile advances of Moses—to keep him from preying on her young daughter—and determined to survive, Mabel flees the Randall plantation. She proceeds through the swamp, following the stars, and finally stops to rest on dry land. For the sake of her daughter, she decides to head back—but is bitten by a poisonous cottonmouth snake and dies in the swamp.

## *The North*

The slave notice at the beginning of the final chapter is for Cora, demonstrating to the reader that she is still free. Ridgeway forces her to lead him to the ghost tunnel. As they descend the steep staircase, she grabs hold of Ridgeway and hurls them both down the stairs. She bangs her head, but so does he, and at least one of his legs is broken. As Ridgeway recites last thoughts for Homer to record, Cora escapes via the handcar. Later she walks, sometimes stopping to sleep, and finally reaches the tunnel's end. Outside the tunnel, a caravan of wagons is passing by, heading west. The last wagon is driven by an old freedman who offers food and welcomes her to ride along.

# Characters

## *Ajarry*

Ajarry is Cora's grandmother. Her village in Africa was raided, and she was enslaved when she was a girl. Her mother was already dead; her father died during the walk to the sea. Ending up at Randall, she had a series of three husbands and bore five children, but only Mabel survived past age ten. Ajarry died from a "knot in her brain"—perhaps an aneurysm, if not a senseless blow.

## *Maisie Anderson*

The daughter of the white family for whom Cora worked in South Carolina seems not to recognize Cora when she sees her later in the museum display.

## *Mr. and Mrs. Anderson*

Cora works for the easygoing Anderson family in South Carolina.

## *Big Anthony*

Big Anthony's fatal three-day punishment for trying to escape sets the stage for Caesar and Cora's escape from the Randall plantation.

## *Ava*

Ava, who is of Mabel's generation, resents Cora's ownership of a garden plot at the Randall plantation. She feels entitled to it because she has a family to feed. Ava arranges for Cora's exile to Hob.

## *Bessie*

*See* Cora

## *Blake*

One of the young men on the Randall plantation, Blake is taken aback at what he sees in Cora's eyes when she demolishes his doghouse. His efforts at tarring her reputation lead up to her rape by Blake's friends. Blake tries to run away but is caught and killed.

## *Boseman*

Boseman is Ridgeway's last loyal white assistant slave catcher. He is shot by Red.

## *Rumsey Brooks*

Brooks is a magnetic young poet who speaks at the Valentine farm.

## *Caesar*

Caesar had lived a relatively privileged life as the slave of Mrs. Garner in Virginia, along with his parents. He was permitted education in woodworking and great freedom of movement. Mrs. Garner promised that she would free them upon her death, but she did not leave a will specifying that, so they remained enslaved. Caesar ends up at Randall but reads secretly (an act forbidden to most slaves) and plots to escape, deciding he needs Cora as a lucky charm, since her mother escaped. In South Carolina, Caesar's alias is Christian Markson. Working in a factory there, he seems to patiently admire Cora, but it turns out he is spending time with another woman friend, Meg. When Ridgeway shows up in town, Caesar is tracked down at the factory, jailed, and then released to a murderous mob and killed.

## *Dr. Campbell*

Dr. Campbell is the first doctor who sees Cora in South Carolina. He gives her a thorough, impersonal exam.

## *Carpenter*

The professional body snatcher with whom Dr. Stevens tags along as a student is Carpenter, a giant Irishman.

## *Chester*

At Randall, Chester is a lively, spunky boy—

until Terrance Randall beats him and then has him whipped for spilling wine.

## *Cobb*

Cobb is Carpenter's assistant.

## *Connelly*

Connelly is the vicious old Irish overseer at Randall.

## *Cora*

Cora is the heart and soul of the novel. Her status as the protagonist is emphasized by the fact that she does not get her "own" chapter headed with her name; the whole book, really, is hers. She shows her essential toughness in multiple ways, such as sending Blake a message by destroying the doghouse that he builds on her garden plot, standing up for Chester despite the beating she was sure to receive, and finally determining, with Caesar's encouragement, to seek her own freedom. That she incidentally kills the boy on the hog trail—purely in self-defense—shows not that she is a murderer but rather that she recognizes the mortal threat represented by white people like him and understands that she must not hold back if she wants to survive. She keeps her wits in South Carolina, not swayed by the whites' campaign for sterilization of former slaves. She survives in circumstances worse than prison in Martin Wells's attic in North Carolina. Her choking Ridgeway into submission is the turning point in the rescue operation in Tennessee. Cora loses far too many friends and helpers in the course of her escape, but even through the massacre at the Indiana farm and Ridgeway's last kidnapping, she survives. If all goes as expected, she will end up in California, as far from the South as can be.

## *Mr. Fields*

Mr. Fields runs the museum in South Carolina and seems not to realize—or care—that it is whitewashing American history to make whites look more benevolent and fair than they actually were in their dealings with other races.

## *Fiona*

In North Carolina, Fiona is the Wells's Irish housemaid. Perceiving the stench in the attic and skeptical of Martin's supposed case of Venezuelan pox, she turns them in under suspicion of harboring a slave. In the community afterward, she boasts of her accomplishment.

## *Mr. Fletcher*

Mr. Fletcher is an elderly, abolition-minded white shop owner in the town near Randall where Caesar tries to sell his woodwork bowls in the market. Mr. Fletcher offers to sell Caesar's crafts at his store as a pretext for offering assistance in reaching the underground railroad. Caesar and Cora reach his house, and Mr. Fletcher successfully navigates through town to bring them to Lumbly's station. Ridgeway reports that Mr. Fletcher's association with Caesar was noticed, and the old man and his wife were killed.

## *Mrs. Garner*

Mrs. Garner promised freedom to Caesar and his family but never granted it. After her death, with his family splintered, Caesar curses her.

## *Georgina*

Georgina, from Delaware, is the teacher at the Valentine farm.

## *Miss Handler*

Cora's teacher in South Carolina is Miss Handler, an epitome of patience.

## *Homer*

A suit-wearing ten-year-old black boy with a bearing like that of a gracefully submissive old slave, Homer is bought and freed by Ridgeway and decides to remain in Ridgeway's service and thus under his protection. He both drives the cart and keeps records of Ridgeway's business dealings and philosophical commentaries.

## *Jamison*

Jamison is the appallingly racist and violent leader of the night riders in the town in North Carolina.

## *Jasmine*

Jasmine was born into slavery in Ethel's family, and the two grew up not unlike sisters, until Ethel's father demanded that they separate. Ethel's dim awareness, during her adolescence, that her father regularly raped Jasmine surely contributed to her suppressed desire to be a savior to Africans. Jasmine bears a mulatto son who looks like his father and like Ethel.

## *Jasper*

Caught in Tennessee, Jasper is slated to be returned to Florida, but his constant singing provokes Ridgeway to kill him.

## *Jockey*

Jockey is a respected elder slave—amazingly, still alive in his fifties—on the Randall plantation.

## *Justin*

The third member of Royal's band, Justin, the one holding the knife, is himself a runaway, and he moves on from Indiana to find his family in Canada.

## *Elijah Lander*

Born free in Boston to a white lawyer and his colored wife, Lander was often ill as a youth but grew up to be an intellectual and noted speaker for the abolitionist cause. The South considers his work seditious, and when the meeting on Valentine farm is ambushed, Lander is assassinated.

## *Lovey*

Cora's best friend is a contrast to her in that she lives exuberantly, even under the yoke of slavery, while Cora is always reserved and withdrawn. Fatefully, she figures out what Caesar and Cora were up to and follows in their escape. Lovey's mother notices her daughter's absence early in the night and causes the alarm to be sounded for all three runaways. Lovey is caught on the hog trail and killed at Randall.

## *Lumbly*

Lumbly is the humdrum station agent who helps Caesar and Cora in Georgia.

## *Miss Lucy*

The proctor at Cora's dormitory in South Carolina, Miss Lucy seems congenial at first, even deferent, but her sense of white supremacy shines through when she tries to enlist Cora as an advocate for black women's sterilization.

## *Mabel*

Mabel is Cora's mother, who escapes the Randall plantation but leaves her daughter behind. All her life, Cora both despises her mother for leaving Randall without her and asks after her, hoping to learn of her whereabouts. In fact, Mabel temporarily escaped and meant to return, but she died from a snakebite.

## *Michael*

Michael was a slave who could recite the Declaration of Independence, though without understanding its meaning. He died on the Randall plantation.

## *Mingo*

A former slave widely admired for having worked hard enough, in his weekend free time, to purchase his wife's, his children's, and finally his own freedom, Mingo is a resident on the Valentine farm. From his privileged position as a legally free man, Mingo can and does scorn runaways—especially so-called murderers like Cora—because they jeopardize the security of people like him.

## *Molly*

Molly is the ten-year-old girl with whom Cora shares a cabin in Indiana.

## *Moses*

A slave enforcer at Randall, Moses is somehow compensated by Ava for sending Cora to Hob. Years before, Moses used threats to force Mabel to submit to his advances, inspiring her attempt at escape.

## *Nag*

A helpful Hob woman, Nag nurses Cora after her whipping.

## *Nelson*

Nelson is the runaway in Missouri for whom Ridgeway fatefully passes through Tennessee.

## *Ollie*

Ollie is the generous, kindhearted old freedman who drives Cora off into the sunset, so to speak, at the novel's end.

## *James Randall*

The elder Randall brother runs the northern half of the plantation with relative forbearance, until he dies of illness.

## *Terrance Randall*

Far harsher than his older brother, Terrance

makes a public spectacle of torturing slaves. He strikes Cora with his cane when she tries to defend Chester, scarring her. When he takes over the northern half of Randall (plantations are referred to in shorthand by the name of the owning family), he intends to force Cora to be his mistress. Her escape thus inspires him to call in Ridgeway, the famed slave catcher, and offer a huge reward for her capture.

## *Red*

A more militant abolitionist than Royal, Red spearheads the use of guns during their rescues, and he kills Boseman. Owing to his embrace of violent means, Red parts ways with the railroad.

## *Arnold Ridgeway*

The slave catcher Ridgeway is ruthless, underscoring his view of runaways as property by referring to any such person as "it." But it turns out he is not entirely devoid of morality, having never owned a slave himself except for Homer, whom he purchased specifically to free, earning the boy's loyalty. Ridgeway also shows some respect for the bodies of captured slave women under his control—he punishes Boseman for intending to violate Cora. He has a philosophical streak, sharing his objectifying, and somewhat objective, views of slaves and the South with Cora as well as with Homer, who writes such things down. When his fall down the tunnel steps with Cora breaks his leg and leaves a bloody gash in his head, he does not rage at Cora but perhaps sees his own end as fitting, and he focuses on giving Homer thoughts to record for posterity's sake.

## *Donald Ridgeway*

Donald is the father of Arnold Ridgeway, the slave catcher. He was a blacksmith who used his talents to get in touch with something very much like what Native Americans call the Great Spirit. Donald's son knew he would never live up to his father's life and career and so opted out of virtuous living.

## *Royal*

Royal leads Cora's rescue in Tennessee after noticing her walking through town in chains. Cora develops feelings for him, and he patiently seeks her affection; he gives her almanacs as gifts, knowing her interest in them. He is the one to first bring her to the ghost tunnel. The two have just reached the point of intimacy where Cora feels comfortable enough to kiss him and let him spend the night (chastely) when the ill-fated meeting at the Valentine farm takes place. Trying to aid Lander, Royal is shot and killed.

## *Sam*

Sam is a jovial, solidly built twenty-five-year-old white man serving as a station agent in South

Carolina. He works at a bar, which helps him learn rumors and news, such as regarding the unethical syphilis study and Ridgeway's arrival in town. His house is burnt down, but he escapes and later finds Cora in Indiana.

## *Dr. Stevens*

Seemingly bright, kind, and respectful, Dr. Stevens nonetheless sends chilling messages when he nonchalantly advises Cora to get sterilized in South Carolina.

## *Sybil*

Sybil is a decade older than Cora and has a daughter, Molly. The three of them share a cabin at the Valentine farm. She is fond of Lander.

## *Gloria Valentine*

Formerly a slave, Gloria was purchased by John Valentine so that he could free and marry her, and she has become an accomplished speaker at the gatherings at their farm.

## *John Valentine*

The owner of the Indiana farm that becomes a haven for runaways has Ethiopian ancestry but often passes as white. He became devoted to helping runaways when ahalf-frozen woman knocked on his door for assistance but died several days later.

Valentine comes to realize that the community must move west in order to survive—but he realizes it too late, as the big meeting is ambushed, the farm buildings destroyed, and many people killed before any move is made.

## *Ethel Wells*

Martin's wife, as a girl, had had dreams of being a savior to Africans, but present-day life in North Carolina leaves her more worried about simply staying alive—which is not guaranteed if she treats any blacks like humans. She is moved to be motherly to Cora when the latter falls ill and her childhood dreams resurface. Ethel allows Cora to remain in a bedroom in the main house as she recuperates, which contributes to her being easily found when the house is searched.

## *Martin Wells*

The wishy-washy son of a just-minded father, Martin ended up following in his father's abolitionist footsteps only because he had thought a map to an underground railroad station was a treasure map. He oversees the closure of the North Carolina station and does not know what to do with Cora when she shows up. His failure to take any risk to get her over the state line leads to her finally being caught and to Martin and his wife's being lynched.

# Themes

## *Slavery*

The reader picking up *The Underground Railroad* on a whim may wonder just what Whitehead has found to say, a century and a half after slavery's end, that has not been said before. As time passes after a historic event like the end of an oppressive institution or a major war, and as more and more stories about the event are told, overlapping perspectives and truisms emerge, and the latest stories must find ever smaller niches to address something original. Yet Whitehead seems to have only the grand picture in mind with his book's title, which seems to address a standardized history of slavery. It is possible that at this point, little that is new can be said about the institution itself, and yet there remain some people—youths and those with insufficient education—who still need the event brought to life for them to truly, viscerally understand it.

Whitehead performs this service, to begin with, perfectly in *The Underground Railroad*. With an unflinching gaze, he unearths every nuance of the enslaved experience in a way that avoids melodrama, the kind of narrative theatricality that leaves straight-talking modern readers at a distance from slavery-era tales like *Uncle Tom's Cabin* (1852). It is almost brutal, how matter-of-factly

Whitehead's narrator relates the most gruesome punishments inflicted on the slaves in Georgia and North Carolina. He offers narrative sympathy where there is room for it, but outright torture is so frequent that elaborate descriptions would risk making the book unreadable. Rather, one appalling violent act after another is rapidly shuffled before the reader's eyes, until the sheer weight of the terrible institution settles squarely on the reader's shoulders.

## Topics for Further Study

- Write a story, perhaps based on an experience in your own life or that of a friend, in which the protagonist is trying to escape a difficult situation and is partly enabled by magical or science-fictional means. Try to ensure that the means in question is not simply dropped into the story as an easy and perfect solution to the difficulty but is something that reflects the complexities of the situation.

- Read *Letters from a Slave Girl: The Story of Harriet Jacobs* (1992), by Mary E. Lyons, a fictionalized version of Jacobs's life told through letters she might have written. Then imagine Harriet and Cora engaging in written correspondence at some point (or at various points) during their lives, whether it is while both are enslaved, after one has been freed, or after both are free. Write at least three such letters for each person.

- Read the online *Complex* article "Why Black People Need Conspiracy Theories" (found at http://www.complex.com/life/2016/10/b conspiracy-theories), by Morehouse College professor David Dennis Jr., as well as any related articles that seem informative and reliable and write an essay in which you summarize Dennis's points and discuss his article in the context of *The Underground Railroad*.

- Using both print and online sources, research one of the issues that are given anachronistic treatments in

Whitehead's novel (that is, placed at a different point in time than they were in reality), including but not limited to lynchings, the Great Migration, sterilization and eugenics, the Tuskegee syphilis study, and independent African American communities—and produce an essay or a multimedia presentation that reflects on the issue and how it signifies the long-term repercussions of slavery.

---

The reader is encouraged to do what the slaves themselves have little choice but to do—get desensitized to the violence, to avoid going crazy with angst over it. And yet at the same time, Whitehead urges the reader to realize that a person would have to be crazy to *not* be affected by all that violence—as the ones who inflicted it arguably were.

## *Racism*

The violence of slavery was rooted in racism. Many whites believed, erroneously—as modern genetic comparisons have shown—that the white race was inherently superior to the black race, offering an excuse for the treatment of Africans as mere property. Whitehead mentions more than once what passes for a moral accounting of slavery among many whites: in Ridgeway's conception, if

Africans "were supposed to have their freedom, they wouldn't be in chains." In effect, this suggests that whatever happens, no matter how terrible, is justified by the fact that it happened. The same reasoning can justify poor treatment of anyone simply because the treatment cannot be defended against—it is an excuse for preying on the defenseless.

Whites in the South developed an institution that treated people as no more than livestock. Sometimes the only way to respond was in animalistic ways—in the biological fight-or-flight dynamic, either running away to escape predatory owners, or standing firm and lashing out at cruel overseers, responding to violence with violence. Yet the very violence resorted to by people at the end of their personal ropes was used to justify characterization of the Africans as violent, unstable, and in need of being treated—and kept—like children. True to life, the racism in the novel comes in a variety of forms, ranging from outright murderous hatred of the black race to prejudicial treatment even among those who do not think of themselves as racist.

## *American Culture*

The overt racism of the slaveholding South is so apparent and unarguable that it needs little illustration to be understood. The villainy of people like Terrance Randall and the overseer Connelly goes without saying. But Whitehead also has a great deal to say about the racism that flourished in American culture even outside of the institution of slavery. The teachers, proctors, and doctors in South Carolina outwardly have the most benevolent intentions—Dr. Stevens, for one, "disapproved of racial prejudice"—but at bottom they all agree that the African American population should be limited as much as possible. Mr. Fields supposedly wants to illuminate the African American experience in his museum but in a way that leaves out the violence, making slaves look contentedly subordinated and whites downright friendly. Similarly, he believes that the museum manages "to illuminate the American experience" merely by having a real tepee appear in the Native American scene—disregarding the broken treaties, massacres, Trail of Tears, slaughtered buffalo herds, and other injustices. The museum's depictions of these scenes are so inaccurate, serve to tell such distorted versions of historical events, that they are effectively false. Elsewhere, the lawmakers in North Carolina are content to allow racially prejudicial laws into the books, and indeed, deliberately prejudicial laws were passed all over the South in the era after the Civil War.

But again, the blame cannot be focused entirely upon the South. More than any other character, Ridgeway, through his musings, whether communicated through the narration or the dialogue, illuminates the misguided nature of the entire American experiment. Regarding the slave patrollers, "in another country they would have been criminals, but this was America." Fundamental to the American attitude is greed, whether for land once held by Indians or for the lives of people from Africa: "Here was the true Great Spirit, the divine thread connecting all human endeavor—if you can keep it, it is yours. Your property, slave or continent. The American imperative." And that very greed was inscribed as the national credo with the concept of Manifest Destiny—America's fate of owning the continent from sea to shining sea.

## *Freedom*

Considering all the ways Cora remains under the yokes of racism and enslavement in the course of her journey away from Georgia, it seems like true freedom might never be attained. The "freedom" she experiences in Martin Wells's attic in North Carolina is in certain ways worse than slavery; at least at Randall, she realizes, she could be out in the field under the sun. But she remains penned in by both the institution she is trying to escape and the nation that hosts it: "Whether in the fields or underground or in an attic room, America remained her warden." Indiana offers the first taste of freedom, but even after receiving news of Terrance Randall's death, she knows that technically, some inheritor or bank somewhere can consider her their property, liable to be claimed. Even at Valentine farm her sense of freedom is limited by the opinions of Mingo and his followers that runaways and murderers, having defied the system instead of working through it, are a liability among the other free blacks. As the novel closes, with Cora catching a ride going through St. Louis, home of the Gateway Arch, to California, Whitehead seems to suggest that what Cora needs most to attain her freedom is distance—physical distance from the people and places responsible for her enslavement, and the passage of time to heal the psychological wounds.

# Style

## *Irony*

The tone of Whitehead's novel is marked by severe irony—a difference between surface and true meaning—at many points, usually reflecting absurd and often hostile views held by white people. When Ajarry is first sold in America, the narrator relates, "A big auction always drew a colorful crowd." Calling the sorts of people who attend a slave auction "colorful" puts a cheery, pleasant spin on their character, but of course those buying slaves are almost universally racist, callous, sadistic, possessive, and selfrighteous—colorful, indeed. The price Ajarry fetches, in turn, is attributed to "that season's glut of young girls." This language is itself callous, reckoning African girls in terms more appropriate to a crop of wheat or the lambs in a flock; the callousness, of course, is not Whitehead's but that of the slavers who gauge human beings in such offhand economic terms. The tone is similarly ironic when the narrator suggests that everyone knew that black people "didn't have birthdays," that Terrance's being cruel to his slaves "was his right," and that for slave catchers "there was no end to their work, the river of slaves that needed to be driven from their hidey-holes and brought to the white man's proper accounting." The ironic note in the last sentence is especially struck with the word "proper," as ludicrously applied to the most morally improper institution ever practiced among humans. Whitehead's use of irony, encapsulated in such dramatically straightforward assertions of what white people believed, but outside of the larger context of the communal white perspective, makes all the clearer how absurd those white beliefs about race and justice were.

## *Postmodernism*

Irony is one hallmark of the postmodern era, when sometimes it seems that nothing can, or should, be taken at face value. Irony can serve the function of holding up a certain perspective so that its flaws become glaringly apparent. The surface value of an ironic statement must be carefully compared with the full sense behind it. Another part of the novel's postmodernism is its use of what might be classified as magic realism, a genre originating in Latin American literature, partly as a response to the disruptions of colonial encounters. Whitehead's use of an actual underground railroad to represent the well-known network of secret rooms, tunnels, and hiding places refreshes the reader's perspective on the history in question in a somewhat ironic way. The reader does not expect an actual train to carry Cora and Caesar through an underground tunnel hundreds of miles long, but when this fantastically or magically happens, the reader can only roll with the narrative possibilities opened up.

Another postmodern means of upending the

reader's perspective is the mixing of genres. In this case, the reader has a familiar genre, the fiction novel, interspersed with what seem very much like nonfictional notices regarding escaped slaves. These notices feature physical descriptions of the slaves, dates, locations, and the full names of the owners, none of whom appear in the novel. Whitehead has in fact confirmed, in an NPR interview, that the notices were gathered from historical records. On the one hand, then, their inclusion enhances the sense of the reality of the novel's action, even as the fantastical element of the railroad brings Cora from state to state. Most strikingly, the fictional novel and nonfictional notices are combined when the last place-name chapter, "The North," is preceded by a notice titled "Ran Away," not lamenting but celebrating Cora's escape. Its ends with the bold declaration, "she was never property." Quite likely no such notice ever appeared in a southern newspaper of the time, but this one makes Cora's destined freedom feel all the more like a blessed actuality.

# Historical Context

## *African American History, Prefigured*

Although the precise time frame of *The Underground Railroad* is not given in the novel, it is said to take place some decades after Great Britain abolished slavery—the slave trade ended in 1807, slavery itself in 1833—and Whitehead related in an interview for NPR's *Fresh Air* that he intended for Cora's escape to be set in the early 1850s. What is fascinating about the novel's historical context, however, is the way Cora's journey through several southern states speaks to other periods in African American history and how race relations founded in slaverypersisted well beyond the end of the wretched institution itself.

## *LYNCHINGS*

Violence toward African American slaves was appallingly common, as Whitehead's novel suggests, but the practice of lynching—often specifically taken to mean hanging, though the term can refer to any fatal mob action—did not become widespread until after the Civil War. Indignant and still angry over the defeat of the Confederacy and the newfound "uppity" attitude of African Americans, southern whites sought ways to punish blacks for perceived transgressions. Given the fact that many of the accusations that led to lynching were entirely invented or falsified, it is not surprising that whites specifically sought ways to murder African Americans without appealing to due process of law. Thus did mob hangings and other killings become all too prevalent through the late nineteenth century and into the early twentieth. Nearly five thousand lynchings took place between 1882 and 1968—and if one imagines all of these people together in one place, the result is something like the "Freedom Trail" in *The Underground Railroad*'s white-supremacist North Carolina. Whitehead has also mentioned that backward echoes of the Holocaust—the coldblooded, institutionalized extermination of a racial population—can be seen in the novel.

## *GREAT MIGRATION*

Although the historical Underground Railroad famously took escaped slaves north as far as necessary to attain freedom—and the only certainty was to go all the way to Canada—this movement did not amount to a chance for African Americans to establish focused communities like Whitehead's Valentine farm in Indiana, which is called "the advance guard of a great migration." What is known historically as the Great Migration took place approximately between 1915 and 1960, when the segregation of the South was a reality of life, and especially when the agricultural economy collapsed during the Great Depression of the 1930s. Urban centers and their relative abundance of industrial and other kinds of work were favored destinations, including Chicago, Detroit, Pittsburgh, and New York. By World War II in the mid 1940s, the push was extending farther west as well, as far as California cities including Oakland, San Francisco, and Los Angeles. Between 1915 and 1960, some five million African Americans migrated from the South to northern and western cities.

## *TUSKEGEE SYPHILIS STUDY*

What was officially called the "Tuskegee Study of Untreated Syphilis in the Negro Male" was begun in 1932. Alabama's Tuskegee Institute was well known since its founding in 1881 by Booker T. Washington as a center of black education. Unfortunately, the institute's leader in the early twentieth century saw fit to allow the US Public Health Service to conduct a study of untreated syphilis there, provided that African American professionals were involved—just one black doctor and one black nurse initially joined the study—and Tuskegee received credit. The intent of the study was to track the course of syphilis if left untreated, in the interest of refining approaches to treatment. The problem was that the African American men enrolled in the study, who believed themselves to have "bad blood," with symptoms including anemia and fatigue, were left entirely uninformed about the truth of the study. They were not told exactly what disease they had and were not offered medication for treatment, even when penicillin became accepted as most effective treatment in 1945. This wildly unethical study—which is mirrored in Whitehead's antebellum South Carolina—did not end until the press finally drew attention to it in 1972. Following court action, some ten million dollars in reparations were extended to the men and families involved.

## Critical Overview

Whitehead has accumulated admiring critics throughout his career, especially for his ability to reinvent genres—and to reinvent himself as a writer—with each new novel. *The Underground Railroad* received almost universally positive attention. In *Kirkus Reviews*, a writer sought to characterize the work by writing, "Imagine a runaway slave novel written with Joseph Heller's deadpan voice leasing both Frederick Douglass' grim realities and H. P. Lovecraft's rococo fantasies"—a combination suggesting how "startlingly original" the novel is. A *Publishers Weekly* reviewer admires the "powerful, precise prose, at once spellbinding and ferocious," and calls the book "literature at its finest" that ought to be required reading for all Americans. In *Library Journal*, Barbara Hoffert affirms that *The Underground Railroad* "raises the bar for fiction addressing slavery." Donna Seaman, in *Booklist*, was effusive, calling the novel "an imaginative, droll, and eviscerating inquiry," a "magnetizing and wrenching saga," and "vividly, often viscerally realistic." The scenes of conflict are "galvanizing," the characters "compelling," and Seaman concludes: "Hard-driving, laser-sharp, artistically superlative, and deeply compassionate, Whitehead's unforgettable odyssey adds a clarion new facet to the literature of racial tyranny and liberation."

*New Statesman* reviewer Randy Boyagoda finds that Whitehead brings the broader story of the injustice of American slavery "to terrible, terrifying new life" in a tale that offers "flatout suspenseful reading" leading up to an "exciting and rending conclusion." Even before Whitehead won the Pulitzer Prize for *The Underground Railroad*, Boyagoda recognized that the novel was Whitehead's "most ambitious and accomplished book, …perhaps his finest work." In the *Spectator*, David Patrikarakos comments that Whitehead tells his tale "beautifully" and artfully—"His gaze takes everything in with neither judgment nor sentiment: his flowing and superb writing, meanwhile, instils both in the reader."

## Compare & Contrast

- **1850s:** The institution of slavery officially persists in America—despite its having already been banned or overturned in places like Great Britain and Haiti—as many people believe that treating another person like property is justified, whether by biblical passages or a cruel "might is right" philosophy

    **Today:** With institutional slavery having ended with the Emancipation Proclamation over 150 years ago, many people believe that slavery is a thing of the past. However, increasing attention is being paid to other forms of slavery in the modern day, especially through trafficking and forced involvement in the sex trade, which occurs even in the United States.

- **1850s:** In the case of an escaped slave or convict, bloodhounds offer the most reliable means—sometimes the only means—of tracking a person down, obtaining the person's scent from clothing or bedding left behind. Notices in newspapers also contribute to search efforts, though physical descriptions are often insufficient for identifying a particular person.

  **Today:** While dogs are still used frequently in efforts to capture wanted convicts or find other missing people, means of detection ranging from fingerprints and DNA testing to photographs, videos, and facial-recognition technology, along with the large-scale distribution of pictures and descriptions made possible in the digital age, all make the recovery of wanted or missing persons more likely.

- **1850s:** The steam locomotive was developed in America in the 1820s and 1830s, and railwaysare laid and extended through the ensuing decades. Though they are noisy and a source of pollution, trains are regarded as impressive marvels of human ingenuity and a prestigious means of transportation.

**Today:** The first American subterranean railway system, or subway, is constructed in Boston, opening in 1897, several decades after the first European subways and a few years before New York's. As for other major underground travel, the prototype is the "Chunnel," the tunnel running under the English channel, though other tunnels, including those in Guangzhou and Beijing, China, are longer.

---

In the *New York Times Book Review*, Juan Gabriel Vásquez calls the novel "striking and imaginative," "as simple as it is bold." He comments that the novel "is carefully built and stunningly daring; it is also, both in expected and unexpected ways, dense, substantial and important." Regarding Whitehead's necessary depictions of violence, Vásquez writes, "He opens his eyes where the rest of us would rather look away. In this, *The Underground Railroad* is courageous but never gratuitous." Regarding the book's magic realist turn, the reviewer states, "Whitehead's imagination, unconstrained by stubborn facts, takes the novel to new places in the narrative of slavery, or rather to places where it actually has something new to say."

And regarding the truths that the novelist manages to convey through his adaptations of factual history, Vásquez comments,

> In a sense, *The Underground Railroad* is Whitehead's own attempt at getting things right, not by telling us what we already know but by vindicating the powers of fiction to interpret the world. In its exploration of the foundational sins of America, it is a brave and necessary book.

In the London *Guardian*, Alex Preston calls Whitehead's effort a "brutal, vital, devastating novel," in which "subtly antique prose and detailed description combine to create a world that is entirely convincing." The literal railroad is seen as "a brilliant conceit," "the spark that ignites the novel," lending it "visionary new life." Preston declares,

> Everything in Whitehead's novel is honed to scintillating sharpness.... I haven't been as simultaneously moved and entertained by a book in many years. This is a luminous, furious, wildly inventive tale that not only shines a bright light on one of the darkest periods of history, but also opens up thrilling new vistas for the form of the novel itself.

Scott Simon of National Public Radio calls Whitehead "one of the most acclaimed young writers in America." Also affirming Whitehead's status, the *Kirkus Reviews* writer concludes, "Whitehead continues the African-American artists' inquiry into race mythology and history with rousing audacity and razor-sharp ingenuity; he is now assuredly a writer of the first rank."

## What Do I Read Next?

- Whitehead perhaps reveals more of himself as both a writer and a person in his earlier novel *John Henry Days* (2001), the tale of a black journalist in New York City—not unlike the author—revolving around the legend of African American railroad worker John Henry. The book was a Pulitzer finalist.

- Whitehead has cited Ralph Ellison's *Invisible Man* (1952), one of the most highly regarded novels in twentieth-century American literature, as a particular influence on him. The tale of a nameless African American foiled by white society at every surreal turn resonates in Cora's path through the several southern states as well as in Whitehead's "tweaked reality" style.

- In *Gulliver's Travels* (1726), by Jonathan Swift, a hapless Englishman finds himself somewhat magically transported from one peculiar place to another, each following its own set of tweaked societal rules. Whitehead has also cited this early novel as an influence on *The Underground Railroad*.

- Now one of the best-known slave narratives, thanks to the popular and critical success of the 2013 film based on it, is Solomon North-up's memoir *Twelve Years a Slave* (1853), which details his being kidnapped and brought south, to spend more than a decade in servitude before finding a way to secure his release. The film stars award-winning Nigerian actor Chiwetel Ejiofor.

- Originally published in 2007 in Canada—where the title proved less controversial than in the United

States—*The Book of Negroes* is Lawrence Hill's drama revolving around a British document known as the Book of Negroes, the record of African Americans who had served the British in the American Revolution and thus merited escape to Canada. In the novel, Aminata realizes that getting into that book is her ticket to freedom.

- *Copper Sun* (2006), by award-winning author Sharon Draper, follows two teenage girls, a slave and an indentured servant, as they escape their Carolina plantation heading not north but south, seeking sanctuary in the Spanish colony in Florida.

- Antagonism between Irish and African Americans is the subject of Walter Dean Myers's 2009 young-adult novel *Riot*. When strife erupts in New York City in the midst of the Civil War in 1863, Claire, with an Irish mother and a black father, finds herself in the middle of things.

# Sources

Boyagoda, Randy, "Catch Me if You Can," in *New Statesman*, December 2, 2016, p. 47.

Gross, Terry, "Colson Whitehead's *Underground Railroad* Is a Literal Train to Freedom," in *Fresh Air*, NPR website, November 18, 2016, http://www.npr.org/2016/11/18/502558001/colson-whiteheads-underground-railroad-is-a-literal-train-to-freedom (accessed August 9, 2017).

"The Great Migration (1915–1960)," BlackPast.org, http://www.blackpast.org/aah/great-migration-1915-1960 (accessed August 9, 2017).

"History of Lynchings," NAACP website, http://www.naacp.org/history-of-lynchings/ (accessed August 9, 2017).

Hoffert, Barbara, Review of *The Underground Railroad*, in *Library Journal*, Vol. 141, No. 12, July 1, 2016, p. 82.

Kennedy, William, "The Yellow Trolley Car in Barcelona, and Other Visions," in *Atlantic*, January 1973, https://www.theatlantic.com/magazine/archive/1973/yellow-trolley-car-in-barcelona-and-other-visions/360848/ (accessed August 8, 2017).

Patrick, Diane, "Tunnel Visions: Colson Whitehead," in *Publishers Weekly*, Vol. 263, No. 30, July 25, 2016, p. 27.

Patrikarakos, David, "A Parable of Good and Evil," in *Spectator*, October 15, 2016, p. 36.

Preston, Alex, Review of *The Underground Railroad*, in *Guardian* (London, England), October 9, 2016, https://www.theguardian.com/books/2016/oct/09/the-underground-railroad-colson-whitehead-revie-luminous-furious-wildly-inventive (accessed August 9, 2017).

"Railroad History, an Overview of the Past," American-Rails.com, http://www.american-rails.com/railroad-history.html (accessed August 11, 2017).

Review of *The Underground Railroad*, in *Kirkus Reviews*, May 1, 2016.

Review of *The Underground Railroad*, in *Publishers Weekly*, Vol. 263, No. 15, April 11, 2016.

Seaman, Donna, "Riding the Underground Railroad," in *Booklist*, Vol. 112, Nos. 19–20, June 1, 2016, p. 37.

Selzer, Linda, "New Eclecticism: An Interview with Colson Whitehead," in *Callaloo*, Vol. 31, No. 2, Spring 2008, pp. 393–401; reprinted in *Contemporary Literary Criticism*, edited by Jeffrey W. Hunter, Vol. 348, 2014.

Simon, Scott, "New Novel Takes 'The Underground Railroad' beyond the Metaphor," in *Weekend Edition Saturday*, NPR website, August 6, 2016, http://www.npr.org/2016/08/06/488969873/new-novel-takes-the-underground-railroad-beyond-the-metaphor (accessed August 9, 2017).

"The Tuskegee Timeline," Centers for Disease Control and Prevention website, https://www.cdc.gov/tuskegee/timeline.htm (accessed August 9, 2017).

Vásquez, Juan Gabriel, "Freedom Ride," in *New York Times Book Review*, August 14, 2016, p. 1.

Whitehead, Colson, *The Underground Railroad*, Fleet, 2017.

# Further Reading

Morrison, Toni, *Beloved*, Alfred A. Knopf, 1987.

> One of the most praised narratives about the turmoils of slavery is this Pulitzer Prize–winning novel by Nobel Prize winner Morrison. The novel sets itself apart from ordinary reality in featuring a ghost.

Walters, Kerry, *The Underground Railroad: A Reference Guide*, ABC-CLIO, 2012.

> Walters's text discusses all aspects of the lifesaving abolitionist network, featuring extensive excerpts of firsthand documents from activists and runaways, as well as those who tried to catch slaves.

Whitehead, Colson, *The Colossus of New York: A City in Thirteen Parts*, Doubleday, 2003.

> Published shortly after Whitehead was awarded his MacArthur Foundation fellowship, this volume of essays introduces readers to both the author himself and the city he calls home.

Willis, Deborah, and Barbara Krauthamer, *Envisioning Emancipation: Black Americans and the End of Slavery*, Temple University Press, 2013.

This book focuses on collected photographs from throughout African American populations in the slavery era, with discussion of what the images signify.

## Suggested Search Terms

Colson Whitehead AND The Underground Railroad

Whitehead AND The Underground Railroad AND prizes

Whitehead AND interview

history of the Underground Railroad

runaway slaves AND legislation

Fugitive Slave Act of 1850

abolitionists AND activism

abolitionists AND rescue efforts

slavery AND magic realism OR fantasy

Printed in December 2024
by Rotomail Italia S.p.A., Vignate (MI) - Italy